THE REDEMPTION OF SCROOGE
YOUTH STUDY BOOK

The Redemption of Scrooge

The Redemption of Scrooge
978-1-5018-2307-7
978-1-5018-2308-4 eBook

The Redemption of Scrooge: Leader Guide
978-1-5018-2309-1
978-1-5018-2310-7 eBook

The Redemption of Scrooge: DVD
978-1-5018-2311-4

The Redemption of Scrooge: Youth Study Book
978-1-5018-2316-9
978-1-5018-2317-6 eBook

The Redemption of Scrooge: Worship Resources
978-1-5018-2320-6 Flash Drive
978-1-5018-2321-3 Download

Also by Matt Rawle

The Faith of a Mockingbird
The Salvation of Doctor Who
Hollywood Jesus

For more information, visit MattRawle.com.

MATT RAWLE

The Redemption of Scrooge

Youth Study Book
by MIKE POTEET

Abingdon Press / Nashville

The Redemption of Scrooge
Youth Study Book

Copyright © 2016 Abingdon Press
All rights reserved.

This book is printed on elemental chlorine-free paper.
978-1-5018-2316-9

16 17 18 19 20 21 22 23 24 25 — 10 9 8 7 6 5 4 3 2 1
MANUFACTURED IN THE UNITED STATES OF AMERICA

CONTENTS

INTRODUCTION

SONGS OF THE SEASON

s any other holiday as full of music as Christmas? Sure, other celebrations get songs. It doesn't feel like the Fourth of July to me until I've heard a nd strike up "The Stars and Stripes Forever." And when Halloween rolls a ound, I dig out an old CD full of "spooky" music—everything from classic c chestral pieces like Camille Saint-Saëns's *Danse Macabre* to pop hits like I y Parker Jr.'s *Ghostbusters* theme. And plenty of people get to hear family a d friends serenade them with "Happy Birthday to You" once a year.

Some hymnbooks include whole sections of songs for the special days a d seasons on the Christian calendar, and most of this music goes unheard c tside church walls. But if you handed a hymnal's Christmas section to some r idom passersby, there's a good chance they'd be able to sing some of the t nes of the hymns, or they would at least recognize some titles.

Music is a major part of Christmas. How many congregations, I wonder, c se their Christmas Eve worship with a candlelit chorus of "Silent Night, I ly Night"? Some churches offer special performances of choral works like

Handel's *Messiah* each December, or hold a Service of Lessons and Carols that is filled with chances to sing familiar favorites. And in the culture at large, you can't escape Christmas music—even if you want to. Carols become commercial soundtracks on TV. Radio stations play a month (or more) of "Winter Wonderland" and "Jingle Bell Rock." Pop stars and celebrities drop new holiday albums every year. In 2015, artists including Kylie Minogue, India.Arie, and KC and the Sunshine Band all released new Christmas albums.[1] More will surely follow in 2016—as of this writing, even William Shatner is recording one![2]

But there's never been a Christmas carol quite like Charles Dickens's *A Christmas Carol.*

DICKENS'S *A CHRISTMAS CAROL*

Published in 1843, the first edition's title page calls the book *A Christmas Carol. In Prose.*—Dickens's nod to the fact that "carols" are poetic lyrics meant to be sung. I haven't been able to find out why Dickens chose to call his "Ghostly little book" (as he refers to it in his Preface) a "carol," but he even went so far in the theme as to call its five chapters *staves*, another term for stanzas.

I wonder, though, if he used this title because Christmas is a season so saturated with song, filled with songs that people enjoy over and over, year after year. Charles Dickens felt it was his duty, as a writer, to increase people's joy. He once said he had "an earnest and true desire to contribute, as far as in me lies, to the common stock of healthful cheerfulness and enjoyment. I have always had, and always shall have, an invincible repugnance to that mole-eyed philosophy which loves the darkness, and winks and scowls in the light."[3]

With *A Christmas Carol*, Dickens delivered a story that has been contributing to the world's "healthful cheerfulness and enjoyment" for over 170 years. If a more joyous ghost story has ever been told, I don't know it. It has proven successful since its first publication, on December 19, 1843; it had already reached its third edition by January 3, 1844, with some nine thousand copies in print.[4] One contemporary review praised it for (among many other

INTRODUCTION

alities) "its impressive eloquence...its playful and sparkling humour...its
ntle spirit of humanity—all of which light up every page, and...put us in
od humour with ourselves, with each other, with the season, and with the
thor."[5]

Playwrights and filmmakers have found *A Christmas Carol* as irresistible as
ders have. The first stage adaptation debuted in February 1844, and there's
en no shortage of versions for stage and screen (both big and small) ever
ce. Some of the more notable include:

- *A Christmas Carol* (1951) starring Alastair Sim—still considered the definitive movie version by many,
- *Scrooge* (1970) starring Albert Finney—a musical version that also features Alec "Obi-Wan Kenobi" Guinness as Marley's ghost,
- *Mickey's Christmas Carol* (1983) starring Scrooge McDuck (who else?) and all your classic Disney favorites (I love the part where Goofy, as Marley's ghost, laments that he is "doomed, doomed for all eternity—maybe even longer!"),
- *The Muppet Christmas Carol* (1992) – Michael Caine (more recently Alfred in the Christopher Nolan Batman movie trilogy) shares the screen with Kermit, Miss Piggy, Fozzie, Gonzo, and the rest of the gang in this creative adaptation,
- *A Christmas Carol* (1999) starring Patrick Stewart – It's Captain Picard and Professor X bringing the "Bah, humbug!" (Stewart had been performing the book as a one-man stage show, just as its author had, for years before he made the movie), and
- *Disney's A Christmas Carol* (2009) – a CGI, motion-capture version starring comedian Jim Carrey as literature's most famous miser.

Whether read in its original form, seen on screen, or simply absorbed
ough cultural osmosis (I saw Scrooge show up in commercials for Honey
it Cheerios as well as my state's lottery last year), *A Christmas Carol*
tivates and delights audiences because it is, as the title of this study says, a

9

story of redemption. It's the story of a new beginning given to the unlikeliest of recipients.

Charles Dickens wrote several other books especially for Christmas, but none of them is more read or more beloved than this one, the tale of how Ebenezer Scrooge found new meaning and purpose in life, and learned lessons from the past, present, and future that helped him "keep Christmas well" all of his days. It's a Christmas carol very few get tired of hearing.

ABOUT THIS RESOURCE

This Youth Study Book is designed to complement Matt Rawle's book *The Redemption of Scrooge*—it follows the same structure and explores some of the same Scriptures and themes—but it can also be used independently.

You will want to create a worship area in your meeting space that contains four Advent candles, perhaps arranged in a wreath (if meeting in a church building, check with responsible parties regarding the use of open flames, and use electric votive candles if needed). If you're using the book as part of a group, decide who will read each of the elements in each session's opening ritual: a reading from Scripture, a reading from *A Christmas Carol*, and a prayer. Everyone can sing or read aloud together the selections from Christmas carols; alternatively, you can find and listen to various versions of the carols online.

A Christmas Carol is widely available in a variety of editions; while you don't have to read it to use this resource, doing so will only enhance your study. You may want to choose a filmed adaptation of the book to watch as part of your study—one listed above, or another of your choosing—especially if you're using the book as part of a group. Giving everyone a common version of the story to react to will improve your sessions.

Use any or all of the suggested activities as time and resources allow, and that match your or your group's interest. Each session contains activities for large and small groups; many of these could also be adapted for individual use.

May God bless your observation and celebration of this Advent season as you study *The Redemption of Scrooge*.

Session 1

BAH! HUMBUG!

DON'T LET THEM CALL YOU SCROOGE!

A few holiday seasons ago, Sedalia, Missouri, resident Kevin Walker decorated his front lawn for Christmas. But Walker didn't set up a nativity scene or an inflatable, illuminated Santa. He decorated his lawn with a Grim Reaper, a tombstone, and a black wreath with *Bah Humbug* in glittery letters.

As you might guess, plenty of neighbors called to complain. Walker told a local radio station the display was his protest of all the commercial hype surrounding Christmas in the United States. But what did the station call him in its coverage? "The biggest Scrooge in America."[1]

Like *Grinch*, the word *Scrooge* has entered our culture's common vocabulary. Even people who've never read *A Christmas Carol* know the term *Scrooge* is used to describe someone who doesn't enjoy Christmas. If you aren't feeling holly, jolly, ho-ho-ho, you'd better keep those feelings to yourself unless you want someone to say, "Stop being such a Scrooge!"

But let's be honest. Not *everything* about Christmas is so great, is it?

Kevin Walker has a point. Did you know that in 2015, the average American planned to spend $882 on Christmas gifts?[2] That's a lot of money for presents given in honor of a baby born into poverty two thousand years ago.

And for a holiday about a "silent night" when "all was calm," Christmas in America sure gets busy and loud. One of the "must-see" holiday highlights near me is a sound-and-light show full of animated toy soldiers and *Nutcracker*-dancing ballerinas, shown on a 2,100-square-foot, high-resolution LED video wall.[3] It's impressive, but hardly conducive to sleeping in heavenly peace.

What drives me craziest about Christmas are those radio stations that interrupt their regular programming for a month (or more) of nonstop holiday songs. Turn on those stations and you'll hear "Jingle Bell Rock" or "Winter Wonderland" for the umpity-umpth time. How many versions of "Let It Snow" does the world really need?

Am I sounding Scrooge-ish yet?

Actually, I enjoy more about the Christmas season than I don't. But I do think our culture makes people who are feeling bad at Christmas feel even worse by insisting that it's the hap-happiest season of all. What about families who can't afford nearly $900 worth of Christmas gifts, because they're struggling to pay the monthly bills? What about people who crave peace and quiet because daily life stresses them out? What about folks who flinch when they hear "it's the most wonderful time of the year" because the loss of a loved one or a job or their health is too recent, too raw?

If you don't happen to feel merry this Christmas, that's okay. Just don't let anyone call you a Scrooge! Because guess what? In *A Christmas Carol*, not even Scrooge is a "Scrooge" the way our culture uses the word. He's actually far worse off—and no one who's already feeling down in December deserves to be accused of being like *him*!

SCROOGE'S WORLD OF ONE

When Scrooge threatens to hit a young caroler who's warbling outside his
office door, he's not just sick and tired of holiday songs. He's lashing out at
what the best of those songs represent.

A little earlier, Scrooge's nephew describes Christmas as "a kind, forgiving,
charitable, pleasant time…when men and women seem by one consent to
open their shut-up hearts freely" (Stave One) to each other, especially to
"people below them" in society. But when this boy "below" Scrooge dares
sing a Christmas song—probably hoping to get a little food or money in
return, as was the custom—Scrooge hears only an unwelcome demand on his
time and resources.

For Scrooge, Christmas is nothing but an intrusion into the world he's
built for himself, a world with a population of one. The narrator tells us
Scrooge likes to "edge his way along the crowded paths of life, warning all
human sympathy to keep its distance" (Stave One). His last name, Scrooge,
was Victorian slang for "squeeze,"[4] and his fixation on money has "scrooged"
everyone else—along with all friendship, love, and compassion—out of
his life.

Scrooge is "a squeezing, wrenching, grasping, scraping, clutching,
covetous, old sinner" (Stave One). His worst sin is the way he shoves other
people aside—human beings who, in his nephew's words, "really [are] fellow-
passengers" (Stave One) through life. When we forget that people around us
are human, especially people less fortunate than we are, we run the risk of
becoming less human ourselves.

A SCRIPTURAL SCROOGE

Scrooge is so miserly with money, you might not notice how much he's
like a rich man Jesus told a story about (see Luke 16:19-31). Unlike Scrooge,
the rich man in Jesus' story spends wealth freely, but only on himself. He
wears robes of purple fabric (very expensive in the ancient world and often
reserved for royalty). He eats lavish feasts daily. He never spares a thought for

Lazarus, the beggar who lies at his house's gate, sick and covered with sores, with only the wild and dirty dogs that lick his wounds for company. Lazarus would have been happy to eat crumbs from the rich man's table, but the man either doesn't know Lazarus is at the door or doesn't care (and neither explanation puts him in a very good light).

Nothing about this sorry situation changes until Lazarus and the rich man both die. Then everything changes. Angels escort Lazarus to a heavenly banquet, where he reclines next to no less a VIP than Abraham, first ancestor of the people of Israel. But the rich man is "tormented in the place of the dead" (Luke 16:23). When the man asks why, Abraham explains that he "received good things [in life] whereas Lazarus received terrible things" (Luke 16:25).

Even now the rich man still thinks only about himself. He begs Abraham to send Lazarus to him with cool water, and to warn his brothers about "this place of agony" (Luke 16:28). Even in his awful afterlife, the rich man is treating Lazarus as less than human, with no identity of his own. He could have bridged the distance between Lazarus and himself when Lazarus was on the rich man's doorstep. Now the gap between them is fixed in Lazarus's favor.

MARY'S CHRISTMAS CAROL

Jesus' story illustrates one of his key teachings about the kingdom of God—one day God's rule will be fully revealed and acknowledged, and God's values and priorities will carry the day. "Those who are last" in this world "will be first" in God's world; "those who are first" now "will be last" then (Luke 13:30; see also Matthew 19:30; 20:16; Mark 10:31). God will not let those who are poor, hungry, and weeping suffer forever (Luke 6:20-21). God will work a wonderful reversal of their fortunes.

That's the message of the "Christmas carol" that Jesus' mother, Mary, sings. When she learns she will give birth, she visits her relative Elizabeth (an older woman pregnant with a miraculous baby, who grows up to become John the Baptist) and sings about what her son's arrival will mean:

With all my heart I glorify the Lord!
    In the depths of who I am I rejoice in God my savior...
[God] has pulled the powerful down from their thrones
    and lifted up the lowly.
He has filled the hungry with good things
    and sent the rich away empty-handed.
He has come to the aid of his servant Israel,
    remembering his mercy....

                            (Luke 1:46-47, 52-54)

Many composers have set Mary's words to music, but I've never heard Mary's "carol" in the shopping malls. Mary's carol reflects different values and priorities. It shifts our focus to those who struggle on society's margins. It promises God will lift up those who are now low and declares that God's kingdom begins to arrive in the birth of Mary's son. If we want to celebrate the birth of this King appropriately, we must pay attention to the people he calls "blessed" (Luke 6:20-21 NRSV). We begin living in God's future world by allowing the people around us, including "the lowly," into our worlds today.

SECOND CHANCE AT HUMANITY, WITH GOD'S HELP

When the ghost of his dead business partner, Jacob Marley, appears to Scrooge, the ghost wears long chains that represent how Marley held back empathy and kindness when still alive. Every failure to lift a finger to help, every time he turned away from someone who suffered, every instance of self-interest at another person's expense—each of these moments added to the length of Marley's chains, link by link and yard by yard.

Marley has learned, too late, that it is not good for human beings to be alone (Genesis 2:18). God created us for community, for connections with other people. Our spirits must, by God's good design, roam beyond the narrow limits of ourselves. That's how we live as human beings.

Using Scrooge's name to scold people who aren't having themselves a merry little Christmas forgets the fact that Scrooge's story is a story of redemption. *A Christmas Carol* is about Scrooge's second chance to become human.

"A merry Christmas, uncle!" his nephew greets him. "God save you" (Stave One). Those are the first words addressed to Scrooge in the book. And by the book's end, Scrooge *is* saved—saved from his self-forged "chains" of greed and indifference, saved from self-imposed exile in a world of one. *A Christmas Carol* never directly says God saves Scrooge, but, as Christians, we believe salvation, in this life as well as the next, comes from no one else.

If someone *does* try to call you a "Scrooge," ask them instead to call you by Scrooge's given name, Ebenezer. *That* name means "stone of help." The prophet Samuel set up a "stone of help" where God gave the ancient Israelites victory over their enemies: "The LORD helped us to this very point" (1 Samuel 7:12). By the grace of God, no one is beyond help. Everyone can be named Ebenezer—*even* Ebenezer Scrooge!

SESSION 1 ACTIVITIES

Gather Around the Advent Candles (Group)

Read aloud:

> The people walking in darkness have seen a great light.
>> On those living in a pitch-dark land, light has dawned...
> A child is born to us, a son is given to us,
>> and authority will be on his shoulders.
> He will be named
> Wonderful Counselor, Mighty God,
> Everlasting Father, Prince of Peace.
>
>> (Isaiah 9:2, 6)

Read aloud:

> I am sure I have always thought of Christmas time...as a good time; a
> kind, forgiving, charitable, pleasant time; the only time I know of, in the
> long calendar of the year, when men and women seem by one consent to
> open their shut-up hearts freely, and to think of people below them as if

16

they really were fellow-passengers to the grave, and not another race of creatures bound on other journeys....I believe that [Christmas] *has* done me good, and *will* do me good; and I say, God bless it!

—Fred, to his uncle Scrooge (Stave One)

Light one Advent candle.

In some congregations, one of the Advent candles represents **peace**.

As Stave Two of *A Christmas Carol* will show us, the Ghost of Christmas Past brings Scrooge a chance to make peace with his own past: to stop struggling against it, to welcome and learn from the lessons its light shows him. Only by accepting the past that cannot be changed can Scrooge find enough peace to move forward and create a better present, for himself and those around him.

The season of Advent looks forward to a day of peace—not only individual, interior peace, but peace between people, even nations, in conflict. In Advent, we look backward to the birth of the Prince of Peace while also looking forward to his return at the end of time, when Christ will finally establish peace over all creation. This "double vision" can bring us the peace we need to speak and act for a better present.

Pray together:

> *God of the past, the present, and time yet to come:*
> *As we remember the ways by which we have come to this day,*
> *We thank you for whatever signs of your presence and help we've seen,*
> *whether dim and faint or blazing bright.*
> *Teach us to count and live out our days as signs of your presence for others.*
> *Make us people who speak peaceful words and live peaceful lives*
> *that all may know Jesus is Emmanuel, God With Us.*
> *And by your Spirit, bless us, every one, this day and always.*
> ***Amen.***

Sing (or read aloud) together:

> God rest you merry, gentlemen, let nothing you dismay,
> For Jesus Christ our Savior was born on upon this day,
> To save us all from Satan's power when we were gone astray.

O tidings of comfort and joy, comfort and joy;
O tidings of comfort and joy.

Now to the Lord sing praises all, you within this place,
And with true love and brotherhood each other now embrace;
This holy tide of Christmas all others doth deface.
O tidings of comfort and joy, comfort and joy;
O tidings of comfort and joy.[5]

—traditional English carol

Large Group Activities

Icebreaker Activity (optional)

In small groups of 2-4 people, take turns rolling a six-sided die. Respond to the prompt below that corresponds to the number you roll.

1 – The Christmas tradition I look forward to the most is _____ because…

2 – One Christmas tradition I've never understood is _____ because…

3 – The strangest thing I do at Christmas time is…

4 – One Christmas tradition I absolutely dread is _____ because…

5 – The person (other than Jesus) I most associate with Christmas is _____ because…

6 – My favorite piece of Christmas music is _____ because…

There are no right or wrong answers! As time and total group size allow, form new small groups and roll the die again for new Christmas conversations.

Watch the Story (video)

Watch whatever portion of your chosen film version of *A Christmas Carol* (see Introduction) corresponds to Stave One of the book (begin at the beginning, and stop when Marley's ghost leaves Scrooge).

Discuss these questions:

- On a scale of 1 ("He just seems like he woke up on the wrong side of the bed") to 5 ("I wouldn't wish this guy on my worst enemy!"), how would you rate this movie's Scrooge for nastiness? Why?
- How does this version portray Christmas as the "kind, forgiving, charitable, pleasant time" Scrooge's nephew says it is?
- How terrifying is Marley in this video? How intense is his interaction with Scrooge, and how does Scrooge respond to him?

Parable Pantomime (Bible study; drama)

Turn in your Bible to Luke 16:19-31. This Scripture contains a story Jesus told. Read the passage to yourself. When everyone has finished reading, choose four people to act it out. One person will be the narrator, while the other three—playing Lazarus, the rich man, and Abraham—will pantomime (act without speaking) appropriate actions as the narrator reads. (You may also want people to play the dogs in verse 21—no real licking, please!—and the angels in verse 22.)

After the show, discuss these questions:

- How do the rich man and Lazarus experience a reversal in this story?
- Why do you think the rich man never helped Lazarus?
- How do you think Jesus wanted to use this story to tell us about God?
- Do you think people who are poor hear this story different from people who are rich? Why?
- What details do you imagine Jesus would include if he were telling this story today?

Mary's "Christmas Carol" (Bible study; music)

Turn in your Bible to Luke 1:46-55. This Scripture is often called the "Magnificat" (mahg-NIFF-ee-caht) after the Latin translation of Mary's first words ("My soul magnifies," verse 46 NRSV). Read the passage aloud, each reader or group of readers taking one verse. Discuss these questions:

- For what specific reasons does Mary praise God in this Scripture?
- What do Mary's words tell us about God?
- What are some specific ways the world will be different when the reversals Mary describes happen?
- How are the changes Mary describes proof of God's "mercy" (verse 54)?

Although the text doesn't specifically say Mary sang her Magnificat, many composers have set her words to music. Search the web for and listen to at least two different versions of the Magnificat, preferably one older and one more recent. (You might also check your congregation's hymnal or songbook to see if it includes music based on this Scripture.) How well does the music in each of these versions communicate the meaning and emotion of the Magnificat?

For an extra challenge, create your own musical setting of the Magnificat! Paraphrase the words to set them to a tune you know, or make up your own melody. Sing with or without instruments. Record your version and post it on your congregation's/youth ministry's website.

Small Group Activities

Dead Nail, Live Energy! (science)

A Christmas Carol begins by stressing that Jacob Marley, Scrooge's business partner, "was as dead as a door-nail" (Stave One). If we don't appreciate that fact, the narrator assures us, "nothing wonderful can come of the story" (Stave One) to follow.

Marley is dead as a door-nail, but he is still used, in ghostly form, to spark a new life for Scrooge. Similarly, in Jesus' day, many Jews thought the old hope of a new king descended from David was dead—but God brought that promise to new life. "A shoot will grow up from the stump of [David's father]

J se," said the prophet Isaiah, "a branch will sprout from his roots" (Isaiah 1 :1). Christians believe that shoot, that branch, is Jesus, whom David's c scendant Joseph adopted and raised as his own son.

You can make an electromagnet out of a nail to remind you of how God t ings new life out of what is dead.[6] You will need:

- One six-inch (15 cm) iron or steel nail (galvanized and aluminum nails won't work)
- 10 feet (3 m) of thin, insulated copper wire
- Pair of wire strippers
- One D-cell battery
- Metal paper clips

1. Strip away a little bit of the insulation at both ends of the wire, exposing the copper beneath.
2. Wrap the wire neatly and tightly around the nail in one direction. Be sure you leave some loose wire at each end.
3. Attach one of the wire's exposed ends to the battery's positive terminal and the other to the battery's negative terminal.
4. You should now be able to use the nail as a magnet to pick up the paper clips.

(IUTION: The wire will become hot quickly, so pick up the paper clips quickly! 1 m't leave the wire attached to the battery for too long.

(ngs Tell the Story (music)

The caroler at Scrooge's door is singing "God Rest You Merry, Gentlemen," a hough he sings the first line as, "God bless you, merry gentleman!" (Stave (1e)—perhaps Dickens deliberately wants us to understand just how much (rooge needs a blessing!

How is the last verse of this carol—the caroler doesn't get to sing it, but y u sang it when lighting the Advent candles in this session—especially a propriate for the themes of Dickens's book?

What is your favorite Christmas carol? How does it tell the Christmas story? In your small group, write a "playlist" of what you think the top three Christmas carols for telling the story of Jesus' birth are. Compare your list with other groups' lists.

Picturing Neighbors to Love (visual art)

Marley's ghost shows Scrooge the dead in torment: not suffering hellfire as the rich man in Jesus' story did, but suffering because they seek "to interfere, for good, in human matters, and [have] lost the power for ever" (Stave One). Sadness and regret torture them.

Look through recent newspapers and magazines for at least one picture of people who are helping someone who suffers. Combine the picture(s) you choose with those chosen by others in your group on a piece of posterboard, butcher paper, or newsprint to make a collage. In the center of your collage, write a Bible verse the group thinks communicates Jesus' call to love our neighbors and to help people who are suffering. Display the finished collages in your church building for the rest of the congregation to see during the Advent and Christmas seasons.

Caroling, Caroling (music; extracurricular activity)

Have you ever gone Christmas caroling? According to *Time* magazine, the tradition isn't as strong as it once was—a development that surely would have disappointed Charles Dickens, who wrote *A Christmas Carol*, in part, to keep the holiday customs he loved alive. "You talk to most baby boomers they might have a caroling story or two," Professor Bob Thompson of Syracuse University told *Time*. "Talk to anybody born after 1960 or so and it's become much less common."[7]

Caroling can be a lot of fun. It can also be a good-natured way to connect with neighbors and tell of your faith. With your parents' or guardians' permission, and with responsible adults' participation, plan and take a caroling trip around your neighborhood or your church building's neighborhood. Rehearse three or four religious carols or hymns that everyone in your group will be comfortable singing. Consider writing your church's

Christmas worship service or information about other special holiday events or religious-themed Christmas cards that you can hand out as invitations at the homes you visit, perhaps with candy canes attached. Gather at a member's house or the church building for snacks when you're done and talk about your experiences.

You might also consider caroling at a local senior citizens' home or in a hospital, with permission from administrators; ask for adult help in arranging such trips.

Closing

Discuss these questions:

- What will you do the next time you hear someone say, to you or someone else, "Stop being such a Scrooge!"?
- What is one specific way you will show sympathy and kindness to one of your "fellow-passengers" through life this week?

Pray this or a similar prayer:

Loving God, open our hearts by the power of your Spirit, that we may walk wherever you lead us, serving our neighbors, especially those who suffer, in mercy and love, for the sake of the poor Child born to save us, your Son, Jesus Christ. **Amen**.

Before the Next Session

- If possible, bring with you next time either a picture that represents one of your earliest Christmas memories or a Christmas ornament associated with a special memory.
- You may want to read Stave Two of *A Christmas Carol*.

Session 2

THE REMEMBRANCE OF CHRISTMAS PAST

PLEASE SIGN HERE, SANTA

was in third grade when I first had doubts about the existence of Santa.

Older kids at school were spreading rumors at recess: Santa didn't come down anyone's chimney on Christmas Eve with presents! A sleigh pulled by flying reindeer? Ridiculous! A North Pole toy factory staffed by elves? Not real!

That year's photo op with "Santa" at the shopping mall was a little weird. If this guy wasn't Santa, I wondered, who *was* he? And were the grown-ups in on this? My mom told me the "Santa's helpers" hypothesis for the first time. Sounded fishy. Santa should hire better help, employees who didn't feel a need to impersonate their boss.

What I needed was proof, one way or the other—and I had a plan to get it.

That Christmas, along with the usual cookies and milk, I left a Christmas card on the hearth for Santa to sign. I could recognize my parents' handwriting, so if either of them tried to pull a fast one and forge Santa's signature, I'd know. But if I saw unfamiliar handwriting on the card the next day, I'd have empirical evidence on my side!

I remember how happy I was to see Santa's autograph that Christmas morning. And I kept the signed card for many years, even after I knew my parents had recruited my aunt, who was visiting us—and whose handwriting they figured, rightly, I *wouldn't* recognize—to sign the card on Santa's behalf. I eventually understood that their solution to my challenge to Santa wasn't meant to trick me, but to give me a fun Christmas memory. It worked.

A MIXTURE OF MEMORIES

What are your Christmas memories like?

Do you smile thinking about late-night Christmas Eve candlelight services and waking up early the next morning to get at the gifts? Do you think about your family around the dinner table, sharing funny stories along with turkey and sweet potatoes; or trekking into the woods—or maybe to a nearby parking lot—to pick out a fresh-cut tree?

Or are your Christmas memories less merry? You spent a holiday season sick in bed, maybe, or a family member spent one in the hospital. Maybe one year, somebody who'd always been able to make it home for Christmas couldn't: the tour of duty wasn't over or the money was too tight for plane tickets or the arguments with loved ones were too recent. Maybe one Christmas fell too close to the death of someone you loved, and no amount of twinkling lights could pierce the darkness you felt.

In Stave Two of *A Christmas Carol*, we discover that Ebenezer Scrooge's Christmases past are a mix of glad memories and sad ones, happy and hurtful ones. We see some "shadows of the things that have been" (Stave Two) in Scrooge's life that are pretty dark. We see him as a young boy, for example, to spend many Christmas breaks alone at his boarding school, while his classmates go home to celebrate. And we see him as a mature businessman, choosing to pursue wealth over his fiancée, Belle, who releases him from their engagement once she realizes Scrooge will never love her as much as he loves money.

But other shadows of the past are brighter. We see the Christmas when Scrooge's sister brings him home for the holidays—because "Father is so much kinder than he used to be, that home's like Heaven!" (Stave Two)—and a Christmas Eve when Mr. Fezziwig, for whom Scrooge worked as a young man, closes his shop early to host a festive night of food, drink, games, and dancing.

The mysterious Ghost of Christmas Past tells Scrooge that this tour of the past is for Scrooge's "welfare" and "reclamation." It's designed to shine light on Scrooge's path through life (and therefore "a bright clear jet of light" shines from the ghost's head) (Stave Two).

You and I aren't likely to be haunted by a ghost like Scrooge's visitor, but, as Christians, we can trust the Holy Spirit—the "Holy Ghost," as the King James Version, the Bible of Charles Dickens's day, says—to use our own mixtures of memories in the same way.

PONDERING OUR PASTS WITH GOD

Even with the seemingly endless, scrollable stream of photos we can see on social media, the old-fashioned photo album hasn't fallen completely out of favor. It's just taking on different forms. GrooveBook, for example, is an app that lets you print one hundred pictures from a smartphone, bound and shipped as a book with perforated pages for easy tearing and sharing. The app's founders, Brian and Julie Whiteman, explain its appeal: "It never gets old having your photos in your hand. It's timeless."[1]

Part of the photo album's timeless appeal is that it calls for us to take a slower pace. When we spend time sitting and really looking at pictures from

27

our past, we can experience something like Scrooge's travels with the Ghost of Christmas Past. We see the people, places, and events that have influenced us, but we can't influence them; those images "have no consciousness of us" (Stave Two). But they can still make us feel joy or sorrow and can lead us to new insights about who we were then and who we want to be now.

For Christians, pictures from our past can also help us understand more clearly when and how God has been with us. Scripture offers many examples of how important memory can be for faith. God commanded the Israelites to celebrate the Passover "for all time" so they and their children might remember how God saved them from slavery (Exodus 12:24-27). Moses told the Israelites that God's identity and commandments "must always be on [their] minds" (Deuteronomy 6:6). The psalm-singer, feeling alone and unloved by God, decides to "remember the LORD's deeds... [God's] wondrous acts from times long past" (Psalm 77:11) and so finds renewed confidence in God.

Because it's Christmas, let's talk about someone in the Christmas story. Mary, Jesus' mother, knew the importance of memory. When the Bethlehem shepherds told the people at the manger the heavenly message they had heard, everyone was amazed, but Mary's reaction ran deeper: she "committed these things to memory and considered them carefully" (Luke 2:18-19). Twelve years later, when Mary and Joseph found young Jesus in the Temple—his "Father's house," he called it (Luke 2:49)—Mary "cherished every word in her heart" (Luke 2:51).

Mary did more than just remember Jesus' birth. She examined those memories for clues to God's will and work, both in Jesus' life and her own. She didn't always understand; there was the time, for example, she and Jesus' brothers and sisters tried to get him to stop preaching because they feared he was "out of his mind" (Mark 3:21)! But when we see her for the last time in Scripture, she's with Jesus' disciples in Jerusalem, praying and waiting with them for the Holy Spirit (Acts 1:12-14).

The way Mary deliberately and devotedly spent time with her memories must have helped shape her faith in her son. Her memories must have helped her realize that, although she was Jesus' mother, she belonged with the group people who called him *Lord*. She must have remained open to God guiding her through her memories—as open as she had been to God's guidance when she agreed to the miraculous plan, all those years before.

LIGHT FROM THE PAST

Christmas can make us more aware than we usually are of how powerful, and sometimes painful, memories can be. The holiday hardwires itself into It appeals so strongly to our senses—bright and colorful lights to see, sweet-smelling and delicious cookies to eat, prickly tree branches and crinkly wrapping paper to touch, carols and other songs to hear and sing—that whatever we feel about it, good or bad, we're likely to feel with special force.

So remembering Christmases past may not always be something we feel like doing. Either we've lived through some Christmases we'd just as soon forget, or we've celebrated some Christmases that were so great, we don't see how this year's holiday could hope to live up. Maybe, like Scrooge, we've had some of each.

That's why Mary's attitude toward memory is what we need, especially at Christmastime. When the Ghost of Christmas Past confronts Scrooge with his memories, Scrooge tries to snuff the ghost out, but he can't do it. The ghost itself vanishes under the "extinguisher-cap," but Scrooge, though he "pressed it down [on the ghost's head] with all his force, he could not hide the light: which streamed from under it, in an unbroken flood upon the ground" (Stave Two).

I love that line: Scrooge "could not hide the light" from his past. It reminds me of a Bible verse we often hear in churches during Advent and Christmas, from the beginning of John's Gospel: "The light shines in the darkness, and the darkness doesn't extinguish the light" (John 1:5). John is talking about a greater light; he's talking about God's Word, God's Son, who "became flesh and made his home among us" in Jesus (1:14). But whenever and wherever the light of truth shines on us, as it can through our memories, we can be sure is a reflection of God's ultimate Light.

Pleasant or not, our past is our past. We can't change it. We can't hide from it. We can only learn from it. Like Mary, we can welcome the light shining from our memories. God shines light so we can see God and ourselves more clearly, and may also see how to grow as those who follow Jesus, the Light of the World.

SESSION 2 ACTIVITIES

Gather Around the Advent Candles (Group)

Read aloud:

> LORD, you have been our help,
>> generation after generation.
> Before the mountains were born,
>> before you birthed the earth and the inhabited world—
>> from forever in the past
>> to forever in the future, you are God. . . .
> Teach us to number our days
>> so we can have a wise heart. . . .
> Let your acts be seen by your servants;
>> let your glory be seen by their children.
> Let the kindness of the Lord our God be over us.
>> Make the work of our hands last.
>> Make the work of our hands last!
>
> (Psalm 90:1-2, 12, 16-17)

Read aloud:

> "Spirit!" said Scrooge in a broken voice, "remove me from this place."
>
> "I told you these were the shadows of the things that had been," said the Ghost. "That they are what they are, do not blame me!"
>
> "Remove me!" Scrooge exclaimed. "I cannot bear it!"

He turned upon the Ghost, and seeing that it looked on him with a face in which in some strange way there were fragments of all the faces it had shown him, wrestled with it....

In the struggle...Scrooge observed that its light was burning high and bright; and dimly connecting that with its influence over him, he seized the extinguisher-cap, and by a sudden action pressed it down upon its head.

The Spirit dropped beneath it, so that the extinguisher covered its whole form; but though Scrooge pressed it down with all his force, he could not hide the light: which streamed from under it, in an unbroken flood upon the ground.

—(Stave Two)

Light two Advent candles.

In some congregations, one of the Advent candles represents **hope**.

A Christmas Carol is a story about a personal hope. As Marley's ghost tells the miser, "I am here to-night to warn you, that you have yet a chance and hope of escaping my fate" (Stave One). Scrooge receives a chance to rejoin the human race; he receives the hope of redemption.

Advent is a season of hope not only for individuals but also for the world. We look forward to the day when God will redeem all creation, transforming it into the world God created it to be, when Christ returns to bring God's kingdom fully and finally.

Pray together:

God of the past, the present, and time yet to come:
As we prepare to celebrate again the birth of your Son,
Keep the light of his blessed star always before us,
Leading us to other people, especially those in need,
In whom we may meet and serve God;
And by your Spirit, bless us, every one, this day and always.
Amen.

31

Sing (or read aloud) together:

Come, thou long expected Jesus,
Born to set thy people free;
From our fears and sins release us,
Let us find our rest in thee.
Israel's strength and consolation,
Hope of all the earth thou art;
Dear desire of every nation,
Joy of every longing heart.

Born thy people to deliver,
Born a child and yet a King,
Born to reign in us forever,
Now thy gracious kingdom bring.
By thine own eternal spirit
Rule in all our hearts alone;
By thine all sufficient merit,
Raise us to thy glorious throne.
—Charles Wesley, 1744[2]

Large Group Activities

Icebreaker Activity (optional)

If you brought a picture that represents one of your earliest Christmas memories, or a Christmas ornament associated with a special memory, show it to the group and briefly talk about it. If you didn't bring a photo or ornament, you can still talk about one of your earliest or most powerful Christmas memories.

Watch the Story (video)

Watch whatever portion of your chosen film version of *A Christmas Carol* (see introduction) corresponds to Stave Two of the book (the visit of the Ghost of Christmas Past).

Discuss these questions:

- How does this production portray the Ghost of Christmas Past? How, if at all, does this portrayal represent something about the nature of memory, or about how the light of the past can shine on the present?
- Why do you think the Ghost of Christmas Past shows Scrooge each of the memories that it does?
- If you could relive any happy memory as vividly as Scrooge remembers Mr. Fezziwig's Christmas party, what memory would you choose, and why?
- What signs do you see that this ghost's visit is starting to change Scrooge?

Mary's "Photo Album" (Bible study, visual art)

Read Luke 2:15-20 and 2:41-52. Mary actively remembers the events of Jesus' birth and childhood.

- How does Mary's careful consideration of her past lead her to insights into what God is doing in her present?
- When has your own remembrance of the past helped you see God's activity in your life or in the lives of others today?

Work with others to create a "photo album" or "scrapbook" Mary might have used (if photography and scrapbooking been hadhobbies in her day!) to "[commit] these things to memory and [consider] them carefully" (Luke 2:19). Collect images—from the Internet, from old Christian education materials your church has on hand (Sunday school leaflets, VBS resources, and so forth), from Christmas cards, from newspapers and magazines—or draw some pictures yourself to depict or represent key events from Jesus' youth. Be ready to talk about how remembering each moment you picture can help us know Jesus and God better, as these memories helped Mary.

33

Always on Your Mind (Bible study, memorization)

Read Deuteronomy 6:4-9. Moses addresses these words to the Israelites as they stand on the threshold of entering the Promised Land, after their forty-year trek through the wilderness. In Judaism, even today, verses 4-5 are known as the Shema, Hebrew for "Listen!" They are "often regarded as the Jewish confession of faith, or creed."[3]

- Why is it important that the Israelites remember the truth in these words as they begin their new life in the Promised Land?
- What practical steps does Moses tell the Israelites to take to remember this truth?
- Read Mark 12:28-34. How did remembering this truth shape Jesus' faith and behavior?
- What memories most powerfully shape your faith in God and your practice as a believer today?

Make and play a memory game to help you memorize verses 4-5. Work with others to prepare a set of cards on which each of the following key words is written on two index cards: *hear, Israel, God, LORD, only, love, heart, being, strength.* Shuffle the cards—you should have 18—and arrange them face-down in a 3 x 6 grid. With other players, take turns turning over two cards at a time. Whenever you make a match, attempt to recite verses 4-5 from memory (other players can check your accuracy against a Bible). If you recite the verses correctly, you win the pair; if not, the pair goes back in the grid. The player who makes and wins the most matched pairs wins the game.

Small Group Activities

Shadow Art (visual art)

The Ghost of Christmas Past tells Scrooge the people, places, and events they witness are "but shadows of the things that have been" (Stave Two). Some of Scrooge's shadows are lovelier than others.

Choose an interestingly shaped Christmas object—a tree-topping star, an angel-shaped ornament, a set of Nativity figures—and place it in front of a light source so that it casts a shadow. Trace the shadow onto a piece of white paper, then decorate it—with crayons, markers, paint, stickers, and whatever other art supplies are available—to make it a lovely shadow. As you work, discuss with others: how can faith in Jesus uncover beauty even in memories that seem like shadows?

Christmas Popsicle Stick Picture Frame (visual art, craft)

Here's a quick and easy craft you may not have made since you were a little kid that can help you sit and really look at a picture from your past. Glue together craft sticks ("popsicle sticks") to make a picture frame. You'll need at least four, glued together at their corners in a square or rectangle, but you can use more sticks if you wish, to make your frame's borders thicker; search the Internet for a phrase like "popsicle stick picture frame" and you'll find plenty of examples to inspire you. Give your frame a Christmas theme by painting the sticks in Christmas colors—red and green, of course, are seasonal favorites in our culture at large, although white and gold are Christmas colors in many churches—or by cutting images out of old Christmas cards to glue onto the sticks. Tape a photo of a Christmas past by its edges to the reverse of the frame. You could glue a length of ribbon or yarn to the back of the frame's top edge to make it a Christmas tree ornament. Whenever you look at the picture in the frame, reflect on how God was present with you at that time, and how God is present with you now.

Music of Times Past (music, movement)

The highlight of Scrooge's time with the Ghost of Christmas Past is the remembrance of Mr. Fezziwig's Christmas Eve party. In the book, the narrator tells us that the Fezziwigs and their guests dance to an old English country tune, "Sir Roger de Coverley." Search for this song on the Internet. Listen to it; watch others dancing to it—and, should the spirit move you, try dancing along yourself! (You don't have to dance it "the right way." Just enjoy the sounds and *move*. Don't worry—we'll never tell!)

What songs do you remember from childhood that you haven't heard in a while? Search for and listen to them online.

- What do you remember and feel, hearing this music again?
- How, if at all, has the passage of time affected the way you hear these songs?
- When and how has God used music to help you grow in faith?

Closing

Discuss these questions:

- What is one specific Christmas memory you want to keep in mind this week, and why?
- What is one lesson you have learned from your past that you will talk to someone else about this week?

Pray this or a similar prayer:

Faithful God, by your Spirit's power, may we see your light in the light that shines from our memories, glimpsing clearly the ways you have led us to this time through your Son, Jesus Christ. **Amen**.

Before the Next Session

- Bring a Christmas snack (store-bought or homemade) to share to the next session.
- You may want to read Stave Three of *A Christmas Carol*.

Session 3

THE LIFE OF
CHRISTMAS PRESENT

"SUCH A GOOSE!"

When I read about the Cratchit family's meager Christmas dinner, it makes me think of a rubber chicken. Why? One December the church I grew up in staged a musical adaptation of *A Christmas Carol*. I played Peter, one of Bob Cratchit's six kids—the one who's wearing his father's "monstrous shirt collar...in honour of the day" (Stave Three) and who's peeking at the potatoes before they're ready to be served (at least, that's how our director told me to play the scene; in the novel, he's simply blowing on the flame so the potatoes will boil faster).

In rehearsals, my fellow Cratchit kids and I had trouble mustering the over-the-top enthusiasm we were supposed to show when delivering the line,

"There's such a goose, Martha" (Stave Three). So our director showed us what she wanted us to do. She jumped up and down and shouted the words while clapping her hands, then spread them wide apart to show how big the family's goose looked in these children's eyes.

I wasn't at all sure the scene was going to work because the prop "goose" our Mrs. Cratchit served was a scrawny, floppy rubber chicken—the kind you might find a circus clown hitting the ringmaster on the head with. I thought the thing looked ridiculous, and hoped our audience wouldn't get a good look at it. Seeing that plastic poultry as *"such"* a goose required a lot of imagination.

JOY IN THE GOOSE GAP

What I didn't appreciate then was that this "goose gap"—the difference between the bird as it actually is and as the Cratchit family sees it—is *precisely* what Charles Dickens wanted readers to notice.

"Such a bustle ensued" when the family brings the goose to the table, says the narrator, "that you might have thought a goose the rarest of all birds . . . and in truth it was something very like it in that house" (Stave Three). According to the BBC, goose was "the meat centerpiece [of Christmas dinner] for a less well-off family where beef or turkey were beyond reach."[1] And the Cratchits have not one speck of their goose to spare: "Mrs. Cratchit said with great delight (surveying one small atom of a bone upon the dish), they hadn't ate it all at last" (Stave Three). Only when it is stretched as far as possible by the applesauce and mashed potatoes is this goose a complete meal for the family.

And yet the Cratchits aren't disappointed in or ashamed of their just-barely-enough holiday meal. They are grateful for it. They are sincerely happy and genuinely joyful around the table. Why?

Carol presents the family's high spirits as one example of the general air of cheerfulness associated with Christmas. Dickens depicts the Ghost of Christmas Present sprinkling incense from a cornucopialike torch over people, their food, and their festivities during the twelve days of Christmas (December 25 through January 5, or Twelfth Night). It's a wonderful personification of how "the Christmas spirit" can make everything seem a little brighter, a little merrier during the holiday season.

But, as the ghost tells Scrooge, "My life upon this globe, is very brief" (Stave Three). And as we've already discussed in this study, the Christmas spirit doesn't always come through, not for everyone. Christians know we need greater strength when life gets hard—because life is hard for the Cratchits, as it is hard for too many people in the real world.

The Apostle Paul knew how to find that strength. When he wrote a letter to first-century believers in the Greek city of Philippi, he had plenty of reasons to feel less than an "air of cheerfulness." His preaching of the gospel had landed him in a Roman prison. He was cut off from his missionary coworkers and from the congregations he cared for. Rival preachers were moving in on his ministry, preaching different versions of the message about the Messiah.

But Paul's letter to the Philippians boils over with joy as surely as those potatoes Peter Cratchit tends to are boiling. "I have learned the secret to being content in any and every circumstance," said Paul, "whether full or hungry or whether having plenty or being poor. I can endure all these things through the power of the one who gives me strength" (Philippians 4:12-13). Because Paul depended on Jesus Christ—"who loved me and gave himself for me," as he said in another letter (Galatians 2:20)—Paul knew a deep joy that didn't depend on what he was facing at any given time. "Be glad in the Lord always!" he urged the Philippians. "Again I say, be glad!" (Philippians 4:4). Paul also encouraged expressions of gratitude to God, promising that joy and thankfulness would allow the Philippians to experience "the peace of God that exceeds all understanding" (Philippians 4:7).

The Cratchits don't make a big show of their Christian faith, but I think their faith is the real reason for their joy and gratitude, despite their economic hardship, despite Tiny Tim's crippling and life-threatening illness. Tim, in fact, tells his father he hopes it pleased others to see him at church, because they might then think about Jesus, "who made lame beggars walk and blind men see." The Cratchit family says grace before Bob carves open the goose, and the Cratchits are "happy, grateful, pleased with one another, and contented with the time" (Stave Three). They seem to have discovered the same secret strength Paul had—that they can endure all things, and endure them joyfully, through the power of Christ.

PAYING ATTENTION TO PEOPLE IN POVERTY

Some cynics say Dickens wrote *A Christmas Carol* just because he needed money. And, yes, sales of his previous book—the inelegantly titled *Life and Adventures of Martin Chuzzlewit*—had been sluggish; and, yes, some of London's literary critics were wondering whether Dickens was losing his shine.

But Dickens's bank account wasn't the only, or even the main, force motivating his holiday ghost story. Once Dickens had the idea for it, a friend to whom he wrote later recalled, he "wept, and laughed, and wept again ... and thinking [about it] he walked about the back streets of London, fifteen and twenty miles, many a night when all sober folk had gone to bed."[7] Dickens felt such excitement about *A Christmas Carol* because he knew it could work a change in readers almost as mighty as the change the story's supernatural visitors work in Ebenezer Scrooge.

The Ghost of Christmas Present's time with Scrooge ends with a scene not always included in movie and TV versions, but it is crucial for understanding why Dickens wrote the story he did. The ghost reveals two "wretched, abject, frightful, hideous, miserable" (Stave Three) children sheltered under its robes. "This boy is Ignorance," says the ghost. "This girl is Want" (Stave Three)— or lack. They are not the ghost's children, but humanity's. The ghost warns Scrooge the children will bring about society's ruin unless society cares for them.

It's a more serious moral than many people realize *A Christmas Carol* teaches, but it shouldn't catch Christians by surprise. We hear a similar message throughout Scripture:

- God commands the freed Hebrew slaves, as they build their new society, to pay special attention to immagrants, because they were once strangers in Egypt (Exodus 22:21; Deuteronomy 10:19).

- God commands Israelite farmers to leave leftover crops for people who are hungry (Leviticus 23:22; Ruth 2:15-16).
- Ancient Israel's prophets call God's people "to share your bread with the hungry, and bring the homeless poor into your house" (Isaiah 58:7 NRSV). Amos, for example, delivers God's stinging rebuke of those who grow fat and rich while neighbors suffer and starve: "Hear this word, you cows of Bashan...who cheat the weak, who crush the needy, who say to their husbands, 'Bring drinks, so we can get drunk!'" (Amos 4:1). (I bet Amos had choice words for gluttonous men, too!) The divine verdict is unrelenting: "Prepare to meet your God, Israel!" (Amos 4:12).

Jesus, too, preached God's care for people in poverty. At Christmas, we remember—if we're remembering the real story, not some feel-good, Christmas-card version of it—that Jesus was born into poverty, with only an animal's feeding trough for a bed. During his life, he had "no place to lay his head" (Luke 9:58). He performed miracles for hungry people; his amazing feeding of five thousand at once is the only miracle, except for the Resurrection, recorded by all four Gospels.

GOD'S GENEROUS JUSTICE

Jesus ate with and preached good news to the poor (see Luke 4:18). And he told stories about them: parables designed to provoke hearers into recognizing the poor as fellow human beings who were precious in God's sight. (As a storyteller, then, Dickens was in fine company!)

Jesus' parable about workers in a vineyard is one of those stories (Matthew 20:1-16). On the surface, it's a ridiculous tale: No manager would pay longtime employees the same amount as rookies who'd just clocked in a few minutes before quitting time. But this isn't a story designed to be a Harvard Business School case study. It's a story about God's extravagantly generous justice.

God's justice is about making what's wrong right, and what's wrong in this parable is the assumption—revealed in the reaction of the laborers who worked in the hot sun all day—that there's not enough to go around, that some are more entitled to life's resources than others. God's justice insists there *is* enough for *everyone*. God denies no one's needs. We can hear the manager's question to the workers as God's question to all those who are materially well-off: "Don't I have the right to do what I want with what belongs to me? Or are you resentful because I'm generous?" (Matthew 20:15).

When *A Christmas Carol* begins, Scrooge has a real resentment problem. Remember what he told those men who were collecting money for charity? He'd rather see people in poverty go to debtors' prison, or be forced to labor in workhouses, or just die and "decrease the surplus population" (Stave One) than have to spend "his" money to support them. But the Ghost of Christmas Present shows Scrooge the urgency of generous justice. The ghost throws Scrooge's earlier, callous words back in his face, confronting him with the same truth found in Jesus' parable: We dare not begrudge our fellow human beings the gifts God has given to all of us. We can only know true joy when everyone does.

And so Scrooge will, once his ghostly visitations are over, decide he can no longer pay Bob Cratchit punishingly low wages. He will decide he must do what he can to get Tiny Tim the medical help the boy so desperately needs. He will feed the Cratchit family, not a goose that looks like a cheap rubber chicken, but a plump, prize-winning turkey. He will be generously just—and so become one of what Jesus calls us to be: "children of [our] Father who is in heaven" (Matthew 5:45), generously giving gifts, withholding what is needed from no one, lavishing the world and its people with the unending resource of love.

SESSION 3 ACTIVITIES

Gather Around the Advent Candles (Group)

Read aloud:

> Shout triumphantly to the LORD, all the earth!
> Serve the LORD with celebration!
> Come before him with shouts of joy!

Know that the LORD is God—
> he made us; we belong to him.
> We are his people,
> the sheep of his own pasture.

Enter his gates with thanks;
> enter his courtyards with praise!
> Thank him! Bless his name!

Because the LORD is good,
> his loyal love lasts forever;
> his faithfulness lasts generation after generation.

(Psalm 100)

Read aloud:

The house fronts looked black enough, and the windows blacker, contrasting with the smooth white sheet of snow upon the roofs, and with the dirtier snow upon the ground.... There was nothing very cheerful in the climate or the town, and yet was there an air of cheerfulness abroad that the clearest summer air and brightest summer sun might have endeavoured to diffuse in vain.

For, the people who were shovelling away on the housetops were jovial and full of glee; calling out to one another from the parapets, and now and then exchanging a facetious snowball...laughing heartily if it went right and not less heartily if it went wrong. The poulterers' shops were still half open, and the fruiterers' were radiant in their glory.... [The] customers were all so hurried and so eager in the hopeful promise of the day, that they tumbled up against each other at the door, clashing their wicker baskets wildly, and left their purchases upon the counter, and came running back to fetch them, and committed hundreds of the like mistakes, in the best humour possible....

[The Ghost of Christmas Present] stood with Scrooge beside him in a baker's doorway, and taking off the covers as their bearers passed, sprinkled incense on their dinners from his torch. And it was a very uncommon kind of torch, for once or twice when there were angry words between some dinner-carriers who had jostled each other, he shed a few drops of water on them from it, and their good humour was restored directly. For they said, it was a shame to quarrel upon Christmas Day. And so it was! God love it, so it was!

—(Stave Three)

Light three Advent candles.

In some congregations, one of the Advent candles represents **love**.

In *A Christmas Carol*, the Ghost of Christmas Present increases the love that people feel for each other. The Spirit sprinkles its special seasoning of love on any meal "kindly given," but on "a poor one most… [b]ecause it needs it most" (Stave Three)—or, as Dickens's original manuscript read, "Because my eldest brother [that is, Jesus] took them especially under his protection."[3]

In the season of Advent, we remember that Jesus came to the world as the ultimate expression of God's love. The Son of God joined humanity—bone of our bone, flesh of our flesh—in the Incarnation. Our whole lives have been hallowed—made holy—by God's presence in Jesus. We proclaim, as the Apostle Paul did, that "nothing can separate us from God's love in Christ Jesus our Lord" (Romans 8:38). And this confidence in the love of God that is ours through Christ moves us to act in love toward others—including those he especially took under his protection, the ones he called "the least of these brothers and sisters of mine" (Matthew 25:40).

Pray together:

> God of the past, the present, and time yet to come:
> Your joy is our strength; your presence, our only true power.
> Gladden us now by making us aware of how near you are,
> and move us to draw near to others, especially the sisters and
> brothers you especially protected when you walked this earth,
> bringing your joy in all we say and do.
> And by your Spirit, bless us, every one, this day and always.
> **Amen**.

Sing (or read aloud) together:

> Love came down at Christmas,
> love all lovely, Love divine;
> love was born at Christmas,
> star and angels gave the sign.
>
> Worship we the Godhead,
> love incarnate, Love divine;
> worship we our Jesus:
> but wherewith for sacred sign?
>
> Love shall be our token,
> love be yours and love be mine,
> Love to God and [others][4],
> love for plea and gift and sign.
> — Christina Rossetti, 1885[5]

Large Group Activities

Icebreaker Activity (optional)

If you and others brought Christmas snacks, pile them together—a reminder of the pile of fine foods the Ghost of Christmas Present brought to Scrooge's room—and enjoy the "feast"! Be certain none of the snacks are wasted. If your group doesn't eat them all, find a way to share what is left with others in or outside of your congregation.

Watch the Story (video)

Watch whatever portion of your chosen film version of *A Christmas Carol* (see introduction) corresponds to Stave Three of the book (the visit of the Ghost of Christmas Present).

Discuss these questions:

- How do the filmmakers communicate a sense of joy in this section of the film?

- Does this version show both the Cratchit family's dinner and the Christmas party hosted by Scrooge's nephew, Fred? If so, what comparisons and contrasts can you make between the two celebrations? If not, why do you think the filmmakers chose to focus on one celebration or the other?

- Does this version include the scene of Ignorance and Want at the end of the Spirit's visit? If so, how effectively do you think the film conveys that scene's message? If not, why do you think the film omits it?

A Puppet Parable (Bible study, performing arts)

Read Matthew 20:1-16 and discuss these questions:

- How do you react to the landowner paying all the workers one day's wage, regardless of how long they actually worked in his vineyard?
- When have you received something you didn't deserve thanks to another person's generosity? How did that experience make you feel?
- When are you most tempted to be resentful of what others have?
- What does this story show and tell us about God's priorities?
- What are the practical, real-world implications this story has for how we live as Jesus' followers?

Make puppets from paper lunch sacks to depict the characters in the parable. Use crayons or markers to draw their faces, fabric scraps to dress them, yarn to give them hair, and whatever other art supplies you have to add the extra touches you wish. (If you want further instructions, check out a website such as http://www.wikihow.com/Make-a-Paper-Bag-Puppet.) Your group will need to create a paper sack "cast" of at least the owner and several laborers; you might also want to make a Jesus puppet to narrate the story. Once the puppets are ready, plan and perform a show for younger children in your congregation. Ask them what they think Jesus' story is all about, and let them teach you something!

Small Group Activities

"Christmas Pudding" (cooking)

Traditional English Christmas puddings like the one the Cratchits eat take a fair amount of time and work, but some simpler alternatives are available. Consider baking one of these recipes that require less time but still result in a tasty treat (or substitute your own favorite Christmas dessert recipe). Enjoy the results yourself, and be certain to bake enough so you have some to share with others!

- Chocolate Plum Pudding Cake (http://allrecipes.com/recipe/7897 /chocolate-plum-pudding-cake/) (about two hours; you'll need to plan ahead some)
- Chocolate Fudge Brownie (http://www.lifestylefood.com.au /recipes/11422/chocolate-fudge-brownie) (about 25 minutes to bake)
- Plum Pudding Cookies (http://www.diabeticlivingonline .com/recipe/plum-pudding-cookies/) (8 minutes to cook, plus preparation time)

"It Is Good to Be Children" (word games; physical movement games)

Evaluating Fred and his guests at their Christmas party, the narrator says "it is good to be children sometimes, and never better than at Christmas, when its mighty Founder was a child himself" (Stave Three). When we keep a childlike sense of fun alive, we can remember that Jesus told his disciples that "whoever doesn't welcome God's kingdom like a child will never enter it" (Mark 10:15). Play one or more of these games played at Fred's Christmas party:

- Blindman's Bluff - Choose and blindfold a volunteer; have them spin around several times; then call out to them and try to keep from getting tagged. (Leave out the "buffeting," or hitting, of the blindfolded person!) The first player tagged becomes the next person blindfolded.

- "I Love My Love with an 'A'" - Players take turns completing a sentence with words that begin with the same letter of the alphabet, starting with "A": "I love my love with an A because [s/he] is _____, took me to _____ and gave me _____." (The first player fills in the blanks with "A" words, the second with "B" words, and so on.)

- "How, When, and Where?" - While one player leaves the room, the others agree on an object the absent player must guess. The absent player returns and can asks three questions: "How do you like it?" "When do you like it?" and "Where do you like it?" (Traditionally, all players are asked each question, but you can shorten the game by having the guesser ask each player only one of these questions.) Words with multiple meanings will work best; read an example using the word "spring" at http://www.waywordradio.org /discussion/topics/the-game-of-how-when-and-where-in-a -christmas-carol/.

- "Yes and No" - Similar to Twenty Questions: "Scrooge's nephew had to think of something, and the rest must find out what; he only answering to their questions yes or no, as the case was" (Stave Three).

Picturing Ignorance and Want (visual art)

Taking images from newspapers and magazines, create a collage of pictures representing social conditions where God's gifts need most to be shared. As you work, discuss with your group what your youth ministry or congregation could be or already is doing to help people living in such situations.

Closing

Discuss these questions:

- What specific gifts from God are you grateful for this Christmas? How will you show that gratitude this week?
- What is one specific action you will take this week to show concern for people who are living with poverty?

Pray this or a similar prayer:

God of joy, by your Spirit may our celebrations of the Savior's birth increase our cheer and confidence in him, and lead us to serve our neighbors with gladness, giving thanks to you at all times for your Son, Jesus Christ. **Amen.**

Before the Next Session

- You may want to read Staves Four and Five of *A Christmas Carol*.

Session 4

THE HOPE OF
CHRISTMAS FUTURE

"What do you want on your tombstone?" That was the question the sour-faced sheriff asked a condemned desperado about to be hanged in a Wild West town square. But instead of uttering some deathless epitaph, the criminal said, "Cheese and pepperoni."

Tombstone frozen pizza's TV ads from the 1990s surprised me. Generally, we modern North Americans don't like being reminded of our mortality. We do all we can to avoid thinking about the fact that—sooner or later, one way or another—the Grim Reaper comes for us all.

Certainly, it comes to Ebenezer Scrooge near the end of *A Christmas Carol*. Scrooge identifies his last supernatural visitor, correctly, as the Ghost of Christmas Yet To Come; but this silent, spooky specter, shrouded in a black cloak and "scatter[ing] gloom and mystery" (Stave Four) as it moves, is just as surely a personification of Death itself. All that's missing is a sickle in its hand.

As if to remove any doubt about its true identity, this ghost guides Scrooge to his own grave. Seeing his name on the neglected tombstone confirms for Scrooge that, if he continues to live a mean, miserly, self-centered life, no one will feel anything but relief and gladness once he's gone.

When, as a kid, I heard the story of *A Christmas Carol* for the first time, the scene of Scrooge collapsing in fear and anguish at his own grave shocked me. It felt like the twist ending of an old *Twilight Zone* episode. It upset me (just as Charles Dickens meant it to upset readers).

The scene still bothers me, but for different reasons. It doesn't feel like a "big reveal" any more. Of *course* Scrooge is the dead man around whom his vision of a future Christmas revolves. Of *course* no one wants to go to his funeral (not even for a free lunch afterward). Of *course* he's the covered-up corpse he sees stretched out on a bed. And of *course* his name is the name chiseled into that tombstone. How could any of it be otherwise?

Here's the hard truth: *Some* "Christmas Yet To Come" will be, for all of us, a Christmas we're not around to celebrate. Maybe—hopefully—it will be a Christmas decades away; maybe it will be the next December 25 that rolls around. But whenever it comes, one "Christmas Present" will be our last, and we probably won't even know it at the time.

Do you know the song, "Have Yourself a Merry Little Christmas"? It originally contained the line, "Have yourself a merry little Christmas, It may be your last..."[1]

How's that for a "ho, ho, ho"?

FACING THE GRAVE WITH HOPE

How do we cope when, like Scrooge, we face the fact of death head-on?

When I was a teen, I was a hopelessly nerdy Trekkie (truth is, I still am), and I remember a "Star Trek: The Next Generation" episode I found very moving. The *Enterprise*'s security chief (Tasha Yar, played by Denise Crosby) is killed in the line of duty. At her funeral, the crew plays a prerecorded holographic message she'd prepared in case the worst happened. In that recording Tasha says, "Death is that state in which one exists only in the memory of others, which is why it is not an end. No goodbyes. Just good memories."[2]

It's a lovely scene—but from a Christian perspective, it's rotten theology! Scripture teaches that death *is*, in fact, an end. When we die, we really and truly cease to exist. Only God is immortal (see 1 Timothy 6:16). We "are dust, and to dust [we] shall return" (Genesis 3:19 NRSV). And as for living on in others' memories? The author of Ecclesiastes cautions, "There is no more reward for [the dead]; even the memory of them is lost" (Ecclesiastes 9:5).

There's nothing *wrong* with hoping people will remember us when we die. But those people will someday die too; and whether and how they remember us is out of our hands. A friend once told me she wanted to be remembered as someone "whose name old men speak with reverence, and young children lisp in awe." She was very poetic, but she wasn't a believer in God, so doing something big and important with her life was, she felt, her only shot at lasting significance.

Christians have a better hope for lasting significance. This hope doesn't depend on anything big and important we do with our lives—it depends completely on the big and important thing Jesus did for us with *his* life.

CHRISTMAS IN HEBREWS

The Book of Hebrews doesn't have the traditional trappings of what we call "the Christmas story." You won't find shepherds watching their flock by night, magi from the East following yonder star, or "little Lord Jesus asleep on the hay." But you *will* find an amazing explanation of why Christmas matters.

The writer announces that God, who has spoken to God's people in a variety of ways in the past, has now spoken "through a Son" (Hebrews 1:2): "the light of God's glory and the imprint of God's being" (1:3), who shared our flesh and blood (2:14) and "isn't ashamed to call [us] brothers and sisters" (2:11).

Think about that. Let that sink in. *Jesus is not ashamed of us*—of you, or me. All the stupid and sinful stuff we do, all the thoughtless ways we hurt ourselves and others and our world, all the times we, like Scrooge, shut our fellow human beings out of our hearts—none of it's enough to make Jesus ashamed of us. The Son of God loves us so much that he became like us so he could die a death like ours and set us free from the fear of death (see Hebrews 2:14-16).

Jesus was born to do a lot of important things—to teach and preach God's message, heal people who were sick, eat with society's forgotten ones, bless little children, challenge authorities and powers that hurt people instead of helping them—but he said the most important thing he was born to do was to die. "I was born and came into the world for this reason," he told Pontius Pilate, "to testify to the truth" (John 18:37). The Greek word for *testify* in that verse is the source of the English word "martyr."[3] With his death, Jesus was a martyr, a witness, to the truth that "everyone who believes in [God's Son] won't perish but will have eternal life" (John 3:16). Or, as Hebrews says, the Son "carried out the cleansing of people from their sins" through his death (1:3), and so leads "many sons and daughters...to glory" (2:10).

Death is an end—but not *the* end. Confronted with his own mortality, Scrooge gets another chance at life. He is freely given a new beginning. Because of Jesus' death and resurrection, so are we. "I was dead, but look!" declares the risen Jesus. "Now I'm alive forever and always" (Revelation 1:18). Those who have faith in him will be able to say the same.

AN ALTERED LIFE

God's gift of new life after our death doesn't depend on our doing anything—but that doesn't mean God wants us to sit around doing nothing! The Letter to the Ephesians says God has "brought us to life with Christ" (Ephesians 2:5) by grace—an undeserved gift, "not something [we] did" (2:9)—because we were "created in Christ Jesus to do good things. God planned for these good things to be the way that we live our lives" (2:10).

A Christmas Carol is a story about salvation, but it's not a story about the hope of heaven. It's a story about experiencing the new, saved, redeemed life in *this* world. When Scrooge wakes up on Christmas Day, he discovers "the Time before him was his own, to make amends in!" (Stave Five). He seizes his chance to make a difference here and now. As he promised the last ghost, he begins to lead a changed life.

54

The only proper response to the promise of eternal life tomorrow is an altered life today! What we do in our altered lives may not be big and important in the world's eyes; it may not earn us a place on history's roll call of heroes. But even small good works can be great ones. Just ask Tiny Tim— "who did NOT die," the narrator assures us (Stave Five), thanks to Scrooge's newfound generosity. Some people laugh to see the change in Scrooge, but he doesn't mind. He's laughing for joy in his own heart. He is at last doing all the good things he was made to do and will do them even if the world thinks him foolish. As the Apostle Paul teaches, "the foolishness of God is wiser than human wisdom, and the weakness of God is stronger than human strength" (1 Corinthians 1:25).

On Christmas Eve, Scrooge dismissed Christmas as a "humbug"—a fraud, a nuisance, a waste of time. But on Christmas Day, he knows how "to keep Christmas well, if any man alive possessed the knowledge" (Stave Five). The narrator fervently wishes, "May that be truly said of us, and all of us!" (Stave Five). That's an especially appropriate goal for Christians. Keeping Christmas well isn't about whether we say "Merry Christmas" or "Happy Holidays." Keeping Christmas well isn't about putting religious stamps on Christmas cards, or making sure Nativity scenes get equal time with Santa Claus at City Hall. Keeping Christmas well *is* about doing those good works that God prepared to be our way of life. It's about doing what civil rights leader and theologian Howard Thurman identified as "the work of Christmas": caring for broken people and a broken world, doing what we can to make peace among everyone, and always "making music in the heart."[4]

SESSION 4 ACTIVITIES

Gather Around the Advent Candles (Group)

Read aloud:

> Nearby shepherds were living in the fields, guarding their sheep at night. The Lord's angel stood before them, the Lord's glory shone around them, and they were terrified.

The angel said, "Don't be afraid! Look! I bring good news to you—wonderful, joyous news for all people. Your savior is born today in David's city. He is Christ the Lord. This is a sign for you: you will find a newborn baby wrapped snugly and lying in a manger." Suddenly a great assembly of the heavenly forces was with the angel praising God. They said, "Glory to God in heaven, and on earth peace among those whom he favors."

When the angels returned to heaven, the shepherds said to each other, "Let's go right now to Bethlehem and see what's happened. Let's confirm what the Lord has revealed to us." They went quickly and found Mary and Joseph, and the baby lying in the manger. When they saw this, they reported what they had been told about this child. Everyone who heard it was amazed at what the shepherds told them. Mary committed these things to memory and considered them carefully. The shepherds returned home, glorifying and praising God for all they had heard and seen. Everything happened just as they had been told.

(Luke 2:8-20)

Read aloud:

"I don't know what to do!" cried Scrooge, laughing and crying in the same breath.... "I am as light as a feather, I am as happy as an angel, I am as merry as a schoolboy.... A merry Christmas to everybody! A happy New Year to all the world! Hallo here! Whoop! Hallo!"...

Really, for a man who had been out of practice for so many years, it was a splendid laugh, a most illustrious laugh. The father of a long, long, line of brilliant laughs!...

Running to the window, he opened it, and put out his head. No fog, no mist; clear, bright, jovial, stirring, cold; cold, piping for the blood to dance to; Golden sunlight; Heavenly sky; sweet fresh air; merry bells. Oh, glorious. Glorious!

—(Stave Five)

Light four Advent candles.

In some congregations, one of the Advent candles represents **joy**.

In *A Christmas Carol*, the story ends with wave after wave of joy as Scrooge, as a result of his night with the Ghosts of Christmas Past, Present, and Yet To Come, rejoins the human race with generous, even extravagant, expressions of care and concern for others. No longer does Scrooge's world contain only himself. His nephew, Fred; his clerk, Bob Cratchit; Bob's son, Tiny Tim (to whom we are told Scrooge becomes like a second father); the gentlemen to whom he refused a charitable contribution the night before—Scrooge's newfound joy in life moves him to embrace them all, doing whatever he can for their good.

In the season of Advent, we talk and sing a lot about joy. True joy, like Scrooge's joy, always directs us outward, toward our neighbors, whether they are our own family or strangers in need. True joy is more than happiness—it is God's gift, and leads us to celebrate and share God's blessings with everyone.

Pray together:

> *God of the past, the present, and time yet to come:*
> *We pray, not for a "merry" Christmas, but for a joyful celebration of the Savior's birth:*
> *A Christmas that, no matter what our circumstances,*
> *refocuses our attention on your self-giving love in Jesus' birth, life, death, and resurrection,*
> *and renews our commitment to follow him.*
> *May we be disciples who serve our Lord and our neighbors with gladness.*
> *And by your Spirit, bless us, every one, this day and always.*
> ***Amen.***

Sing (or read aloud) together:

> Joy to the World, the Lord is come!
> Let earth receive her King;
> Let every heart prepare Him room,

And Heaven and nature sing,
And Heaven and nature sing,
And Heaven, and Heaven, and nature sing.

—Isaac Watts, 1719[5]

LARGE GROUP ACTIVITIES

Icebreaker Activity (optional)

So, what would *you* want on *your* tombstone? (We're not talking pizza this time!) On an index card, write two words that you would want others to remember you by. Don't write your name on the card. Put your card together with everyone else's in a bag. Take turns withdrawing a card and guessing who wrote it.

Watch the Story (video)

Watch whatever portion of your chosen film version of *A Christmas Carol* (see Introduction) corresponds to Staves Four and Five of the book (from the Ghost of Christmas Yet To Come's arrival until the end). Discuss these questions:

- What details about the final ghost and its visit to Scrooge do the filmmakers emphasize, and why?
- How effectively do you think the film portrays Scrooge as a changed man? Why?

Create a Christmas Cross (Bible study, craft activity)

Although Hebrews 2:10-16 doesn't make any direct mention of Jesus' birth, it's an important Scripture for understanding why Jesus was born and the difference his life makes. Read the passage and then discuss these questions:

- What's so important about the fact that Jesus was a real human being who really suffered?
- What difference does Jesus' death make for us?
- What does a life lived free from fear of death and the devil look like?
- What glimpses of the "glory" (verse 10) to which Jesus is leading us have you already seen?
- What does it mean to you, personally, that Jesus is not ashamed to call you brother or sister?

To make a visual reminder of the connection between Jesus' birth and Jesus' death, tightly wrap two large craft sticks (6 x 3/4 inches) in Christmas gift wrap. Place one stick on top of the other in the shape of the cross. Secure the sticks with glue, or tie together by crisscrossing the sticks' intersection with yarn or gift ribbon.

Practice Lectio Divina (Bible study, meditation)

In *A Christmas Carol*, Scrooge doesn't spend the rest of his days doing good works in order to earn his redemption, but in grateful response to having received it. Ephesians 2:1-10 talks about the same relationship between God's grace and our good works. Read this Scripture using an ancient form of Bible study and prayer known as *lectio divina* (Latin, "divine reading"). Many methods for *lectio divina* exist, but they all offer a contemplative encounter with God's Word through the words of the Bible. It is an approach to "Bible study" that engages not only the head but also the heart.

Here's one pattern for you to follow with your group:

1. Recruit three different readers.

2. Reader 1 reads the passage aloud. Participants listen for a word, phrase or image that catches their attention or grabs their imagination— something from the Scripture that "shimmers" for them.

3. After about a minute of silence, participants name aloud what "shimmered" for them, without comment or further discussion.

4. Reader 2 reads the passage aloud. This time, participants think about how the passage intersects their life. They may reflect on what "shimmered" for them in the first reading, or another word, phrase or image may attract their attention this time. They may visualize themselves in the passage, responding to whatever sensory language it contains. Spend 2-3 minutes of silence asking yourself and asking God, "What in these words connects with my life?"

5. Participants talk briefly about their reflections on the passage. Others may ask short questions for clarification, but don't have long conversations yet.

6. Reader 3 reads the passage aloud. This time, participants think about this question: "What is God calling me to do or be through this Scripture?" Spend a few minutes of silence thinking about what specific action you will take or attitude you will adopt as a result of hearing God's Word in this passage.

7. Participants talk about what they sense God is calling them to do or be and discuss their reflections with each other.

Small Group Activities

Twelve Days of Good Works

Traditionally, the church has observed Christmas not as a single day, but as the twelve-day season of Christmas. It begins at midnight on Christmas Day and continues until January 5, the eve of Epiphany. All too often, the only reminder in our culture of "Christmastide" is the song, "The Twelve Days of Christmas." Once December 25 comes and goes, most of society is ready to move on (the stores are already decorated for Valentine's Day!).

You can observe Christmastide this year by planning a schedule of specific good works. Each day of Christmas, do one of the "good things" that God planned "to be the way that we live our lives." Use this space to plan your season of grateful response to God's gift in Jesus Christ—and then "keep Christmas well" the rest of the year, too!

December 25 –

December 26 –

December 27 –

December 28 –

December 29 –

December 30 –

December 31 –

January 1 –

January 2 –

January 3 –

January 4 –

January 5 –

Alternative Gift-Giving

To finish our study of *A Christmas Carol,* make a plan with your small group to raise money for a charity or ministry of your choosing. You may not be able to raise an amount that would stagger the charitable solicitor in Stave

Five ("My dear Mr. Scrooge, are you serious?"), but any amount collected and given in love is pleasing in God's sight. "In this way we remember the Lord Jesus' words: 'It is more blessed to give than to receive'" (Acts 20:35).

The opportunities are plenty, especially in your own community, but here are a few national and international suggestions to start your brainstorming:

- **The Heifer Project** – "working to end hunger and poverty around the world by providing livestock and training to struggling communities" (heifer.org)
- **Imagine No Malaria** – "the United Methodist church-wide effort to overcome malaria in Africa" (umc.org/how-we-serve/imagine -no-malaria)
- **Food for the Poor** – an "interdenominational Christian ministry [that] serves the poor in 17 countries throughout the Caribbean and Latin America... provid[ing] food, housing, healthcare, education, fresh water, emergency relief, micro-enterprise solutions and much more" (foodforthepoor.org)

Closing

Discuss these questions:

- What part of Ebenezer Scrooge's story will you remember most? Why?
- What is a new insight you've had about Christian faith as a result of our study?
- What is one good work you will do this week to share God's love?
- How, specifically, do you plan to "keep Christmas well" all year long?

Pray this or a similar prayer:

God of love, by your Spirit may we keep Christmas well, that the world may know and give thanks with us for the great gift you have given in your Son, Jesus Christ. **Amen**.

NOTES

INTRODUCTION

1   Bill Lamb, "Top 10 New Christmas Albums for Gift Giving," *About Entertainment*, October 14, 2015, http://top40.about.com/od/Christmas-Pop-Music/tp/Top-10-New-Christmas-Albums-for-2015-Gift-Giving.htm.

2   Joseph Rose, "William Shatner on Portland, feuds and his Christmas album," *The Oregonian/OregonLive*, February 11, 2016, http://www.oregonlive.com/geek/2016/02/william_shatner_talks_portland.html.

3   Michael Patrick Hearn, *The Annotated Christmas Carol: A Christmas Carol in Prose* (New York: W.W. Norton & Company, Inc., 2004), xxxvi.

4   Ibid., li.

5   *The Illustrated London News* (December 23, 1843), cited by Hearn, *The Annotated Christmas Carol*, lvi.

SESSION 1: BAH! HUMBUG!

1   Kaleb Filis, "The Biggest Scrooge In America Lives In Sedalia," *92.3 Bob FM*, December 9, 2014, http://923bobfm.com/the-biggest-scrooge-in-america-lives-in-sedalia/.

2   American Research Group, Inc., "2015 Christmas Gift Spending Plans Up Slightly," November 21, 2015, http://americanresearchgroup.com/holiday/.

3   "The Comcast Holiday Spectacular," http://www.visitphilly.com/museums-attractions/philadelphia/the-comcast-holiday-spectacular/.

4   Hearn, 8, note 4.

5   "God Rest You Merry, Gentlemen," http://gbod3.org/musicdownloads/GodRestYouMerryGentlemen.pdf.

6   Find video of this exercise: "How to Make an Electromagnet" (http://sciencewithkids.com/Experiments/Energy-Electricity-Experiments/how-to-make-electromagnet.html); "How do I make an electromagnet?" (http://education.jlab.org/qa/electromagnet.html) or "Electromagnet: a fun, at home science experiment" (https://www.youtube.com/watch?v=gH3JoBFyhD8).

7   Kristi Oloffson, "Brief History: Christmas Caroling," *Time*, December 21, 2009, http://content.time.com/time/world/article/0,8599,1949049,00.html.

SESSION 2: THE REMEMBRANCE OF CHRISTMAS PAST

1   Samantha Chapman, Danielle Genet, and Alexa Valiente, "'Shark Tank': Where Are They Now," *ABC News*, May 2, 2014, http://abcnews.go.com/Entertainment/shark-tank-now/story?id=23421719.

2   "Come, Though Long-Expected Jesus," http://www.hymnary.org/text
    /come_thou_long_expected_jesus_born_to.
3   Matt Stefon, *Judaism: History, Belief, and Practice* (New York:Rosen Publishing
    Group, 2012), 124.

Session 3: The Life of Christmas Present

1   Sarah Treanor, "The Costs of Christmas Past and Christmas Present," *BBC
    News*, December 20, 2013, http://www.bbc.com/news/business-25305032.
2   Hearn, xxxiv.
3   Hearn, 92.
4   Original text was "all men." See Christina Georgina Rossetti, "Love
    Came Down at Christmas," Hymnary.org, http://www.hymnary.org/text
    /love_came_down_at_christmas.
5   Ibid.

Session 4: The Hope of Christmas Future

1   Chris Willman, "The history of a popular holiday song," *Entertainment
    Weekly*, January 8, 2007; http://www.ew.com/article/2007/01/08/history
    -popular-holiday-song.
2   "Skin of Evil," teleplay by Joseph Stefano and Hannah Louise Shearer;
    http://www.imdb.com/title/tt0708776/.
3   *Strong's Exhaustive Concordance of the Bible Online*, s.v. "martus," accessed
    June 10, 2016, http://biblehub.com/greek/3144.htm; also *Online Etymoline
    Dictionary*, s. v. "martyr," http://www.etymonline.com/index.php?term=martyr.
4   Adapted from Howard Thurman, "The Work of Christmas," as cited in
    Steven W. Vannoy, *The 10 Greatest Gifts I Give My Children* (New York: Simon
    and Schuster, 2014), 147; http://bit.ly/1O3nnj0.
5   "Joy to the World lyrics," http://www.carols.org.uk/ba27-joy-to-the
    -world.htm.

Made in the USA
Lexington, KY
02 November 2016